good deed rain

Books by Allen Frost

Ohio Trio
Bowl of Water
Another Life
Home Recordings
The Mermaid Translation
The Selected Correspondence of Kenneth Patchen
The Wonderful Stupid Man
Saint Lemonade
Playground
Roosevelt
5 Novels
The Sylvan Moore Show
Town in a Cloud
A Flutter of Birds Passing Through Heaven:
A Tribute to Robert Sund
At the Edge of America
Lake Erie Submarine
The Book of Ticks
I Can Only Imagine
The Orphanage of Abandoned Teenagers
Different Planet
Go with the Flow: A Tribute to Clyde Sanborn
Homeless Sutra
The Lake Walker
A Hundred Dreams Ago

A HUNDRED DREAMS AGO
by Allen Frost

A Hundred Dreams Ago ©2018
Allen Frost, Good Deed Rain
Bellingham, Washington
ISBN 978-1-64204-539-0

Writing: Allen Frost
Cover Illustration & Chapter Illustrations:
  Aaron Gunderson
Back Cover Photo: Author many moons ago
Cover Production: Katrina Svoboda Johnson
Apple: TFK!

"Life is a beautiful, magnificent thing
even to a jellyfish."

  —Charlie Chaplin

A HUNDRED
DREAMS AGO

INTRODUCTION

It's been wet and cold here too; but wonder of wonders, the sun is shining just now.

That's what the poet Knute Skinner over in Ireland told me as I was finishing this manuscript. This is a winter book, written while it was wet and cold, but luckily inspiration wasn't far away.

Back in the days of being a boy, I had a rusted metal box-shaped shortwave radio. As I dialed between the hum and static, I could tune in London, Luxembourg, Berlin, Moscow, and beyond. Somehow I was able to capture their message out of the air. The progress of this book wasn't much different. For 3 cold, wet months I waited for the next transmission and kept record of them on paper. I'd like to present these 109 messages to you now, in hopes that wherever you are the sun is shining (unless it's nighttime of course).

Allen Frost
Bellingham, Washington

A HUNDRED DREAMS AGO

Part 1:
The Blue Remains..............................16

Part 2:
Meanwhile, in the Planetarium.........48

Part 3:
Donald Sleep......................................98

CONTENTS

The Blue Remains
Leaves
A Snail
For a Walk
Imaginary Horses
Falling Rain
The Snail is Gone
Night Rain
The Mice
A Long Distance Call
The Weight of Pigeons
A Deer
Colder Weather
October Sunshine
Another Deer
Sunny
Side Effects
A Hummingbird
Good Luck Woodpecker
Crow Cane
The Grass Grown
Paper Sack

The Bluebird
The Bluebird II
The Spider
Yellow Lion
A Candy Bar
Halloween
House For Rent
4 Ravens
Bird Burial
First Snow
Warmer
Snow
The Winter Pears
Overlooked
The Deer Jumps
Far Enough
Winter Roses
Our Street
5:30 AM
What Happens Next
Sometimes
A Trapped Leaf
Always Amazed
Rain Has Returned
Hold Your Hands Open

Hold A Poem
Confused By Cars
That Morning
Raven Over
Selling Blue
The Snowman
My Job
My Umbrella
A Lantern
One Crow
When the Wind is Done
Two Sleds
Lost Dog
Winter Window
The Path
Salmon Parking Lot
Hawthorn Lights
The Lightbulb
A Perfectly Reasonable Explanation
The Winds
Out of the Rain
Dizzy
The Cedar
A Deer Movie
The Day Owl

Meanwhile, in the Planetarium
The Balance
Charlie Chaplin Dream
Dianne's Miniature Father
Walking Home from the Planetarium
A Baltimore Bird
The Grasshopper
The Bobcat
The Animals
The 1942 Birds
New People
Gorilla Girl
The Hoop Snake
Morgan's Dragon
A Winter Room
The Couch Mermaid
The Phone Booth
The Forbidden City
Our Garden
Speechless
Dianne & the Fake Santa Claus
Hover
A Montana Mouse
The Rhinoceros
Fidelity Lane

The Memory of a Hundred Year Old Boy
The Unfinished Boat
Blue Overalls
The Planetarium Tilt
The Dreamer
Secondhand Unicorns
The Celebrity
The Carol Fund
A Baseball Game in the Planetarium
A Retired Conductor
The Record Player
Donald Sleep

PART 1: *The Blue Remains*

The Blue Remains

Opening
a mussel shell
with a quick
pocket knife

what a sight
when he ate it
in one bite

and tossed
the blue remains
onto the rocks

Leaves

falling
at night
caught in
headlights

A snail
on the door
open and shut
hanging to it
while I go out

She doesn't mind leaving
she takes the rain
for a walk

Imaginary Horses

She brought each one
to this vacant lot
and let them go

If you see them too
she will introduce you

Falling rain
stops and sound
turns into birds
in the air between
our houses

The snail is gone
only raindrops spotting
the white painted door

Night rain
tapping the roof
joining other rivers

The mice
in my dreams
live under floors
scurry behind walls
and worry the scenery

A Long Distance Call

Geese in flight
kept together
by talking

The Weight of Pigeons

Pinned in a row
they slump the wire
like bird laundry

A deer
peacefully crosses
the sunlit road

Colder weather —
there are still some flowers
but the bees are sleeping

October Sunshine

For a while
brighter than leaves
on the ground

Another Deer

The way his feet
stepped in leaves
almost silently

Sunny
everything still
wet with diamonds

Side Effects

She stands
like a ladder
legs splinting her up
and she is yellow
yellow as the sun

Her tail is wagging
all pain is gone
and she is happy
happy with a world
no one else can see

A hummingbird
puffed up flower
full of nectar
catches its breath
by the feeder

It's supposed to be good luck
to have a woodpecker knock
on your house like a salesman
here to wheedle his way in

Crow Cane

The lamppost
with a crow
on top the handle

The Grass Grown

The grass grown
shaggy like a winter
Shetland pony's fur

I don't care
I'll tell the lawnmower
leaned in the garage
to rest and let cobwebs
tie it down

"They told me I have to ask everyone—
Do you want a paper sack for only 5¢?"
She's been cashier so long I wonder
if she is enchanted and needs me
to buy one.

The Bluebird

He ordered glasses
to correct his vision.
Now he doesn't see
the cage he is in

The Bluebird II

The Bluebird is also
the name of a boat
and a memory
sad as the Titanic.
If it wasn't on a trailer
pushed into the hedge,
it was out on Lake Washington,
hitting each wave
so the wooden hull shudders
towards a fate sinking
in Polaroid colors.

The spider moved
along the bathroom wall
to a slightly better
neighborhood

Each day
there's less
yellow lion
in the tree
and more of him
on the ground

She brings him
a candy bar
asking for
heartbreak

Girls pass by
the Halloween boys
the swish of dresses
footsteps in the street
and whispers
on either side

House For Rent

The lights
shine all night
in empty rooms

Four ravens make a merry-go-round,
circle me twice, tilting and cawing
over a roof and gone.

Bird Burial

A spoon shovel
a pocket of earth
for a bird and a flower

First Snow

The moment
you open
the curtain

Warmer

Way above me
a witch flew with the geese

You can't blame her for
wanting somewhere warmer

When she gets there
she will plant her broom
like a palm tree

Snow that held
branches down
thumps on the roof

The Winter Pears

The winter pears
out of my reach
like light bulbs

but along a branch
movement

a squirrel
with 20 watts
in its mouth

Overlooked

The trail of leaves
leading up between
snow covered ferns
stops at the blue sky
on top the hill

such beauty in the world
so obvious it can be overlooked
like the bright red trees
that line our streets below
or the yellow leaves
falling with new snow

The deer jumps
the low blackberry
knowing it is safe
on the other side

Far enough now
from the leaf-blower
I hear a distant crow

Winter roses
none of them
paying attention

Dilly remembers
a farmhouse was there
a barn, and all that was field
and fifty years ago
we knew everyone
along our street

It's 5:30 AM
instead of words
this should be a dream

What Happens Next

He's the one I saw
stepping on leaves
and now he's chasing
a doe across the parking lot
where the power lines
and asphalt converge
the light of cars
windows glow
I hope they know
enough of this world
to get through
what happens next

Sometimes
walking the dog
the woods are quiet
I can feel the eyes
the held breath
animals are waiting
until we go

A trapped leaf
on the creek
while underneath
the current
flows

Always amazed
by hummingbirds
they seem to run
on electricity
half wind
half battery

Rain has returned
rowed in old boats
tossed over wooden sides

Hold your hands open
get used to the rain
the way trees do

Hold a poem
all night
in the morning
write it down

Confused by cars
the surf sound of I-5
a seagull cries

That morning
a long time ago

Raven
over our street
stops on the
totem pole
top of a tree

Selling Blue

It's almost Egypt
the saltwater marsh
tall green reeds
sunlight pulled by tides
home to blue heron
snowy egret and dragonflies

Parked by the view
there's a station wagon
tailgate stacked with blueberries
and someone sitting nearby
in a fold-up chair
selling blue

The Snowman

All last week
I kept the snowman
repaired as he melted and aged
and tried to go underground

Monday morning
I look for him
on a green lawn

My job is raking leaves
bringing them back
to the tree where they started

Under the tree by the bus stop
my umbrella is gone
all the leaves have dropped

Walking home
with a lantern
my silver thermos cap
catches the light
from every passing car
and shines it back

One crow
a black leaf
blown from the tree

When the wind is done shaking our tree
fir cones and broken branches
a badminton birdie

Two sleds in the shadows.
If it doesn't snow again
they can wait for next year.

Lost Dog

A worried panic on its face
legs that blur like
clockwork

Don't ask for
        too much
The sun
        in the winter window

The path has seen more shoes
flattening the leaves into dirt
in a hurry to get there

PART 2: *Meanwhile, in the Planetarium*

Salmon Parking Lot

All this green so close to the road, cedar and firs covered in moss. Can you imagine swimming to this place from the ocean, pushing against the current, waterfalls, finding pools to rest in? The creek isn't far, it sounds like tires on the freeway. We get there and right away we see three salmon parked and blending with the stones.

Hawthorn Lights

Now I know we made a mistake when we dug up the hawthorn tree, when we fought it out of the ground, and like a witch it scratched and used its thorns on us. Even though we replanted it in the backyard, it refused to grow and withered into a charred slump.

After years in this neighborhood, I understand. I have seen where the orchards used to be, old fruit trees mixed among the new growth woods, or on the edge of properties, half hidden by blackberry, behind new houses, where barns fell down. They are still there in an almost unbroken circuit.

Held on sharp branches stretched to the sky, those red berries are beacons, and like the landing lights of airports, they are markers placed in forgotten lines, guiding memory to the ground.

The Lightbulb

Today the lightbulb above the stove burnt out. It died. All the mornings it was alive I would make tea and coffee and a piece of toast and the rest of the kitchen stayed dark except for the spotlit stage. Halfway through the day, I'm still affected by it. If I could write more about it, I would.

A Perfectly Reasonable Explanation

Every morning on the way to the office, I'm just in time to witness a woman putting her dog in a baby carriage. Day after day I tell myself there is a perfectly reasonable explanation.

The Winds

The winds don't only blow the leaves and rattle the roof, they are also getting inside of us and knocking thoughts around and playing with our controls like a spinning carnival ride. After it's gone, people will wake up in the calm and wonder what happened.

Out of the Rain

The movie theater has been abandoned for years and the parking lot has been slowly turning into a meadow again. Along the wall where the ticket window is boarded up, there are sleeping bags and the homeless will sleep there until the police come along to move them.

Dizzy

They were at an amusement park 35 years ago and she wanted to ride the Ferris Wheel, but rides made him dizzy so he stayed on the ground. He watched her go up and around and each time she passed him she would smile and wave and he would smile and wave back. How romantic.

The Cedar

Small enough to grow inside a house, the cedar in a jar leans toward the window light. Time moves slower for a tree. It's taken days to go that far. Though it seems to like being here with us, I wonder what it will remember when it's tall.

A Deer Movie

A deer crossed the road in front of me and I slow the car. Sure enough, another deer follows, running before the windshield like a movie of a deer.

The Day Owl

He doesn't think the night will ever end, taking on the dark, searching the neon lights of this atmosphere, as each jukebox song carries him flying, closer to the dawn.

Meanwhile, in the Planetarium

Every time the class went, it would be pandemonium. With the lights out, there would be gum thrown, boys hopping over chairs, punches on arms, the girls watching out for hands, the teacher's voice barely heard pointing out stars that were projected on a ceiling already spit-balled with constellations.

The Balance

When she stands, she creaks, one back leg spindly and weak as a twig. She does her best and she has learned the balance to live with it and if she meets another younger dog on the path, she hops and pretends there are no years that have weathered her sore.

Charlie Chaplin Dream

Chased by a hundred old-time cars, into the trees with Charlie Chaplin ahead of me, I know this is a dream. So why am I worried? There are worlds within worlds and we can always get away.

Dianne's Miniature Father

This would have been back in the early days of television when the sets were wooden cabinets and the pictures swam in them like shadows. Her father was on the news being interviewed and she took one look at him in that box and ran from the room. He wore his dark suit and his glasses shined from the studio lights, but nobody could hear what he said over the sound of the vacuum cleaner she carried, pointed at the TV to pull him out.

Walking Home from the Planetarium

I made a discovery. It's night and I have to navigate beyond sight, confident that this path will not fall off the edge of the world. I know there is a tree beside me, but only the pale leaves are visible—the few that are still hanging on. They stagger about it like planets in orbit.

A Baltimore Bird

Baltimore is a long way from here and sad as you are, I know one thing is true. You will see the morning before I do. And somewhere—you may have to search for it—there will be a bird who lives only to sing for you.

The Grasshopper

There is so much winter color that I am shocked by our visitor. A lime green grasshopper. I had to get close enough to see those tiny hands, roughened from pulling weeds in the unforgiving weather, clenched to the aluminum whorls of our door, cold as a tractor's skin.

The Bobcat

Our neighbor saw a bobcat in his yard this morning. He showed me the photograph he took on his phone. I can't get it out of my mind. Later on, when I'm walking the dog in those same woods, I'm half hoping to see it, half not.

The Animals

I'm always wondering about the animals left in the vanishing wild: birds, insects, rabbits, coyote, deer, and all the other ones who hide from us. What do they think of us so quickly taking away their world? They seem to be quiet, but their voice is already sewn to ours, waiting to be heard.

The 1942 Birds

The 1942 birds in the old movie are singing from black and white trees. Over by the window, the cage shakes as our blue canary sings back to them.

New People

New people have moved in next door. The kitchen looks lived in now. I can see bananas on the table. I wonder when they will eat them?

Gorilla Girl

It was our one big chance at an old fashioned carnival show when we were in Ohio, at the boat basin where there were tents and tables and flags and crowds and the chanting barker kept calling us in, "Gorillagirlgorillagirlgorillagirlgorillagirl…"

The Hoop Snake

How lucky they got to see the garden snake. Curled up in the winter sun like a hoop left over from summer.

Morgan's Dragon

"I can't find my dragon," Morgan said. She left it on the landing to the second floor. That was days ago. I got my key and we opened doors in case it wandered. Who knows? It's a big castle but you can't blame a dragon for wanting more. They need the sky and mountains and miles to roam.

A Winter Room

There's someone who lives in the woods. A hundred feet from the path in the alder and thorns, a bright blue tarp is wrapped on the ground. Everything is wet and cold in a winter room with no walls, no roof, no thermostat or bed, in a house as big as the planet.

The Couch Mermaid

What does she want? To remain there, under a blanket, with a seashell to her ear. We care to her every need and hope one day the tide will do its work. The ocean is just down the street, calling her.

The Phone Booth

Why do they keep that phone booth? I've never seen anyone in there like the old days, with a handful of change and the meter running like a taxi cab of words. It holds down the corner of the 76 gas station where the tar runs out and I bet if someone pushed it aside, the parking lot would roll back in a rush. You would see the earth again, the roots of trees running cables through the ground, and an old cracked familiar voice would be calling you on the line.

The Forbidden City

Another dream in that marketplace, big as the Forbidden City. I like being there. A green statue walks past me, an old soldier carrying a horse on his back. There's almost too much to see. I'm surrounded by sculptures and sand dollars crackle on the ground. I go to the booksellers—there are rows of them—and that's where I find this book. I want to buy it but it costs more money than I have and part of me knows, I learned a long time ago, you can't take something out of a dream: all you keep is a fading memory.

Our Garden

She wasn't my wife yet but I knew she would be. We were together all the time. The city was our garden we would wander every day. But anytime we tried to leave, the bus drivers would go on strike, or the train would stop when a mudslide would block the track. Once we tried to drive to Seattle in her little blue car. Not far out of town, the highway was shut down. People in helmets directed us off and we soon got lost on a road that took us winding up into forest to a ridge where every living tree disappeared. They had been slaughtered and thrown in piles and the clearcut went on for miles. There was an actual terror in the air, a great buffalo sorrow as real as the ghost of the American Wild West.

Speechless

Working at a movie theater in San Francisco, sometimes he had the chance to meet the stars in person. The night they showed *The Narrow Margin*, Marie Windsor appeared. A line in the lobby led to her. He joined the slow flowing autograph river until he stood before her. She asked him his name. Something 80 years couldn't take from her, that something in a girl's eyes that makes them so different you wish the world was their way. Whatever it is, they radiate and make you fall in. He didn't know what to say. She really had stepped right out of those films and he lost the power of speech. When she handed him the paper with her name on it, he felt he was as close as he had ever been.

A Montana Mouse

There wasn't much to say. I could barely hear her anyway. She lives in Montana and it's cold. Even after she hung up the phone, she kept looking out the window. Sometimes the wind rattled the door and winter would let itself in.

The Rhinoceros

I know it's cold outside but we can't bring him in. He can't fit through the door. Big as a car parked in our yard, we covered him in blankets and laundry and a sleeping bag. He seemed content. I gave him a candle but he ate it.

Fidelity Lane

He always took me somewhere we weren't supposed to go, like construction sites, or sewer tunnels, abandoned buildings and factories locked on Sundays, squeezing around the gate. Fidelity Lane was just one more place we went. If it wasn't for the tipped cement, the rain soaked walls and shadows, we never would have gone.

The Memory of a Hundred Year Old Boy

It's a long way across the ocean, further than any stone thrown at the horizon. He watched the ships in Boston Harbor for years before he found out.

The Unfinished Boat

He left an unfinished boat in the cellar. There were tools, wood, a bag of screws and paint—all it was missing was him.

Blue Overalls

In two blue overalls, they set up ladders and open hidden latches full of wires. They're here to make repairs on the dream machinery. If it doesn't work right tonight they'll hear about it in the morning.

The Planetarium Tilt

The planetarium spends most of its time like any other building. It's got a parking lot and sun on its ordinary walls. But even in daylight it makes its own night. The projector aims at something bigger than a stage or screen. All those chairs are tilted for looking up at the universe.

The Dreamer

A long time ago, before radio, word of him spread like bird songs. The one who crosses deserts, the one who walks on water, has learned to control his dreams. He knew his life was just another dream and more than that, he knew we're all starring in it too. So he kept telling everyone, wake up, everything I do you can too. He could control reality, make miracles and cures, raise the dead, or move mountains if he wanted to. But he knew even life in a dream will have to end. He told us when it would happen and it did.

Secondhand Unicorns

She only has one for sale but she swears it's as good as new.

The Celebrity

He was supposed to be there, the TV star, our town celebrity. His daughter is in the orchestra with my son and I made sure we sat in the back row where I heard he would slip in when the lights dimmed. He didn't. He couldn't free himself from those distant Hollywood lights. But the very next week, I was at the supermarket. It was around 8 PM, when most people are home. I was tired from a long day at the office, but I had to get eggs and bread. Then something caught my attention and made me turn from the gossip magazines and gum. There he was in the next checkout line, making small talk with the cashier. He looked around and saw me and I looked away. He must be used to that. We aren't the famous ones. He paid, took his bag and was gone. In our ordinary world, he looked like someone pretending to belong.

The Carol Fund

Carol, the lady at the corner convenience store has cancer. Read the plastic tip jar on the counter. Whatever you can give will help her. When Dilly was there, he admired the aloe vera plants in the window, competing for attention with the neon beer signs. He asked her for a starter which she gladly gave. Now he wonders what he can give her in return. Once summer rolls around again he grows plenty of cabbage, corn, beets and lettuce in his garden. And wouldn't she love a jar of the blackberry jam he makes every year? Not to mention all the sunshine that comes after winter.

A Baseball Game in the Planetarium

Almost empty, nearly quiet. There's a custodian who sweeps the rows and plays a transistor radio.

A Retired Conductor

He used to raise his arms and when the music began the orchestra turned into a shipyard and the wood and brass would become the shape of some windblown sailing vessel floating above. He can still hear them. They fill the sky around him.

The Record Player

I spent a lot of time in record stores. I suppose I was a sort of John Audubon, out in the fields and the lonely wilds of America. Wherever I lived, my room was lined with vinyl and the songs I played would paper the walls and spin round the place until an open window could be found. Out there were sidewalks, jobs and coffee shops and I was looking, always looking for her. Maybe I was the bird and I was the one singing Sad Songs and Waltzes and when we did finally meet, we were birds together in a shared bed listening to Hawaiian guitar.

PART 3: *Donald Sleep*

This story takes place a long time ago when you could look out your window at night and see silhouettes of trees and the red light on top the Space Needle.

Just before you fell asleep, you would wait for that strange visitor to knock on someone's door and sometimes if you were lucky, it would be you.

Houselights were on, the sidewalk glowed like a river, and Donald Sleep had his choice where to go tonight.

Was it strange to see a grown man in pajamas walking along the sidewalk? No, not at all, the neighborhood was used to him.

There was no mention of his mind, madness or otherwise, he depended on us and we gave him rest.

It's hard to imagine him in our world today. It's hard to believe that people would put up with him now. Would you?

His feet scuff the ground like fallen leaves. What is he carrying? It's a record. Which one is it tonight? Yesterday it was The Speeches of Winston Churchill.

Houses are grown on either side of him, the dark street in between, the fluorescent lamps overhead. Moths flutter around and children stand in windows watching for him.

The neighborhood is like some board game: the blocks, the sidewalks, the houses, complete with obstacles like Barking Dog: Go Back 5 Spaces. What will he roll, where will he land?

There's even an owl on this street who knows Donald Sleep. The owl hoots twice and Donald turns and walks and waves up at the dark tree in the yard.

Did he have a home or apartment or a room of his own? Why did he only appear with the night? Did he have nothing to do with daylight? There are so many questions we will never have answers for.

Which house will he choose? It's like watching a cloud, wondering where he will go. Some nights he has a bed, sometimes it's a couch or a cot, sometimes it's the swing on the porch. All he really needs though is a record player.

What happens when he visits one of these homes? Just watch. The night is a sort of routine. Only the bedtime story is different.

Donald Sleep wants the whole world in on his act when he sets the mood. Before he goes to sleep, he puts a record on and he always gets the dream he wanted.

In those days I had some records too—a 45 single of "Seasons in the Sun," my Robin Hood soundtrack, and the one he would like to play, Peter and the Wolf.

Nowadays you can find the records he liked in Goodwill. It seems so strange that people used to play them—they're so big, heavy, with bright colors and words, and the LPs inside are black and shiny as coal.

Records used to be just about everywhere. I was always drawn to them. Follow the smell of Woolworth's yellow popcorn machine, past the row of plastic red and blue chairs, the Blizzard machine and don't forget down the aisle was the pet section. They sold music over there. They had a cut-out bin where you could buy an album for a dollar.

Sometimes I think I'll find some trace of him. Maybe I'll see him in a junk store, on a record sleeve, standing wobbly before a microphone: Donald Sleep & His Lullaby Orchestra.

Even I can't recall him for sure. I don't know if my memory of him in our living room is just a picture formed from listening to my mother tell me his story. But I seem to see him clearly—standing there in his pajamas, holding a record, with a pillow and blanket folded at the end of our couch.

I guess he's gone back where he started from, back where he was the king of evening.

Our neighborhood was just a vacant lot he needed to pass through on the way to dreamland.

Is that where he vanished to? A world that hums like a beehive deep in the night—the place so many people forget once they're awake.

If I can remember to, the next dream I have, I'll ask around. He's bound to be on someone's couch, or a hammock in a garden where the moon shines and all the flowers spin like records.

A HUNDRED DREAMS AGO
by Allen Frost
Written October 2017—December 2017

Books by Good Deed Rain

Saint Lemonade, Allen Frost, 2014. Two novels illustrated by the author in the manner of the old Big Little Books.

Playground, Allen Frost, 2014. Poems collected from seven years of chapbooks.

Roosevelt, Allen Frost, 2015. A Pacific Northwest novel set in July, 1942, when a boy and a girl search for a missing elephant. Illustrated throughout by Fred Sodt.

5 Novels, Allen Frost, 2015. Novels written over five years, featuring circus giants, clockwork animals, detectives and time travelers.

The Sylvan Moore Show, Allen Frost, 2015. A short story omnibus of 193 stories written over 30 years.

Town in a Cloud, Allen Frost, 2015. A three-part book of poetry, written during the Bellingham rainy seasons of fall, winter, and spring.

A Flutter of Birds Passing Through Heaven: A Tribute to Robert Sund. 2016. Edited by Allen Frost and Paul Piper. The story of a legendary Ish River poet & artist.

At the Edge of America, Allen Frost, 2016. Two novels in one book blend time travel in a mythical poetic America.

Lake Erie Submarine, Allen Frost, 2016. A two week vacation in Ohio inspired these poems, illustrated by the author.

and Light, Paul Piper, 2016. Poetry written over three years. Illustrated with watercolors by Penny Piper.

The Book of Ticks, Allen Frost, 2017. A giant collection of 8 mysterious adventures featuring Phil Ticks. Illustrated throughout by Aaron Gunderson.

I Can Only Imagine, Allen Frost, 2017. Five adventures of love and heartbreak dreamed in an imaginary world. Cover & color illustrations by Annabelle Barrett.

The Orphanage of Abandoned Teenagers, Allen Frost, 2017. A fictional guide for teens and their parents. Illustrated by the author.

In the Valley of Mystic Light: An Oral History of the Skagit Valley Arts Scene, 2017. Edited by Claire Swedberg & Rita Hupy.

Different Planet, Allen Frost, 2017. Four science fiction adventures: reincarnation, robots, talking animals, outer space and clones. Cover & illustrations by Laura Vasyutynska.

Go with the Flow: A Tribute to Clyde Sanborn. 2018. Edited by Allen Frost. The life and art of a timeless river poet.

Homeless Sutra, Allen Frost, 2018. Four stories: Sylvan Moore, a flying monk, a water salesman, and a guardian rabbit.

The Lake Walker, Allen Frost 2018. A little novel set in black and white like one of those old European movies about death and life.

A Hundred Dreams Ago, Allen Frost, 2018. A winter book of poetry and prose. Cover and illustrations by Aaron Gunderson.

www.ingramcontent.com/pod-product-compliance
Lightning Source LLC
LaVergne TN
LVHW041642060526
838200LV00040B/1679